Contents

Smell this

You have five senses that give you all kinds of information about what is going on around you.

The five senses are sight, touch, taste, smell and hearing. This book is about your sense of smell.

Your sense of smell helps you to enjoy your food.

This flower smells nice.

There are smells all around you. What can you smell now?

Most flowers look pretty and are nice to smell. What smells do you like?

A dirty dishcloth looks horrid and smells bad too! What smells don't you like?

Smelly warnings

You often don't think about smells unless they are very strong. But smells can give you important warnings.

Smoke has a very strong smell. The smell of smoke can be a warning. It makes you think of danger. Is something on fire?

◀ Firefighters wear masks to protect their noses and mouths from smoke.

A bad smell warns you when something could harm you.

Rotten food smells bad so you don't want to eat it!

YUM! Smells good!

Most food smells delicious and helps you to feel hungry.

A good sniff!

When you **sniff** deeply, smells in the air go up holes in your **nose** called **nostrils**.

Tiny hairs at the back of your nose sense the smells and send a message to your brain. Your brain tells you what you are smelling.

That smells tasty.

8

Dogs have a much stronger sense of smell than you. They can smell things you can't.

Police use **sniffer dogs** to help them find things.

Activity

Put some smelly cheese (or anything with a strong smell) on a plate. Ask a friend to hide it in a room.

Can you find the smelly cheese by sniffing it out?

Blocked nose

When you have a cold your nose gets blocked up. Smells can't go up your nose so you can't smell very well.

You probably don't mind not being able to smell bad smells!

◀ When your nose is blocked, you also miss smelling good smells.

If you have a cold, you may not be able to smell food properly. This means you might not feel very hungry.

Make a list of things you often smell. Which smells would you miss if you had a blocked nose?

	Would miss	Wouldn't miss
Curry	✔	
Toothpaste		✔
Soap	✔	
Dirty socks		✔
Chocolate	✔	
Oranges	✔	

What's that smell?

Your brain remembers smells you have smelled before. The first time you smell a new smell, it seems very strong and you notice it immediately.

You have to see what is making the new smell to know what it is. When you smell it again, you remember it.

I know that smell...

12

It's harder to recognize a smell when you can't see what it is coming from.

Put some lemon, chocolate, cheese, soap, toothpaste and handcream in six plastic cups. Cover the cups with circles of card punched with holes. Move the cups around then sniff the lids.

Which smells can you recognize?

13

Clean and dirty

You can smell if someone is clean or dirty. What would you smell like if you didn't wash for a week?

▲ When you do a lot of running or playing you can get very dirty.

You smell good when you have had a bath and washed your hair.

14

Dirt with a bad smell is often full of germs that can make you ill.

What can you do to keep your home clean and smelling fresh?

▲ Cleaning makes things smell fresh and helps to get rid of germs.

◀ Bag up smelly rubbish and put it in the bin.

Outdoor smells

I can smell hay and sheep.

We call the air around us outside **fresh air**.

I can smell fish and seaweed.

Smells in the countryside, by the sea and in the city are very different.

I can smell traffic fumes and hot-dogs.

You can tell where you are just by sniffing!

What else might you smell in the countryside, the seaside and a city?

Indoor smells

The air inside your home is full of smells. There are different smells in each room.

What are the strongest smells in your home?

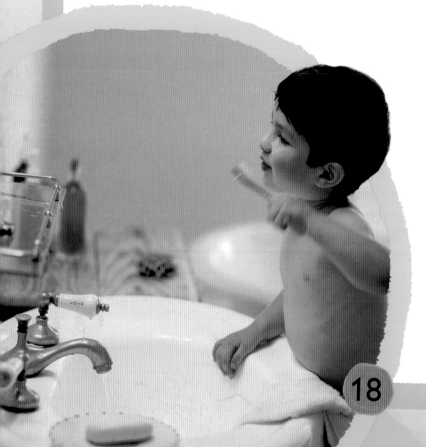

▲ Can you smell food and cooking in the kitchen?

◀ Can you smell shampoo and soap in the bathroom?

Sometimes you can tell what room you are in just by the smell.

Stand somewhere in your home. Shut your eyes and ask someone to turn you round and round, so you don't know where you are.

Ask them to lead you into different rooms. Give a good sniff. Does the smell tell you which room you are in?

Animals and smell

Animals use their sense of smell in all kinds of different ways.

◀ A mother deer can smell her own baby in a big herd.

▶ A shark sniffs blood in the water and then swims towards it to find food.

◀ A cat sniffs its food carefully before it eats it, to make sure it is not bad.

Butterflies follow the smell of flowers to find **sweet** juice called nectar to drink.

Activity

- Collect petals of flowers with a sweet smell.
- Collect leaves of herbs such as mint and lavender.
- Lay them out on some paper to dry. Mix them together gently and put them in a pot.

The **pot pourri** will make your room smell sweet.

Glossary

Fresh air

We call the air outside fresh air. You can open a window to let fresh air into a room.

Nose

Your nose is the part of your body that you smell with.

Nostrils

The two holes in your nose are your nostrils. Air goes into your nostrils when you breathe and sniff.

Pot pourri

A mixture of sweet-smelling petals and leaves.

Sniff

When you sniff, smells in the air go up your nose. You sniff when you want to smell something.

Sniffer dog

A sniffer dog is trained to use its strong sense of smell to find things.

Sweet

Flowers, fruit and soap smell sweet. Sweet smells are usually nice smells.

Index

Parents' and teachers' notes

- Talk about smelling things safely. Smoke and gases can be poisonous. Don't spray anything up your nose. Fine powders such as talc or pepper could damage your nose.

- Ask your child to draw a picture of their face smiling, surrounded by pictures of smells that they like. They can also draw a picture of their face frowning, surrounded by smells they don't like. Talk about why they like some smells and dislike others.

- Make a smell chart. Collect drawings of things with smells that are sweet, delicious, disgusting or give a warning. Sort and stick them onto four large sheets of paper. Make a collection of words to add to the pictures that describe how they smell.

- When you go out, encourage your child to notice and recognise smells in the air around them. Look at pictures of different places such as a farm, the seaside or a city. Talk about what you might smell in these places.

- You can learn new smells. Add pinches of herbs and spices to drops of cooking oil (to stop powder going up your nose). Smell and name the different herbs and spices. Which ones can your child match to the packets they came from?

- Collect pictures of animals with different-shaped noses. Look for their nostrils. Discuss how they use their noses to breathe and smell.

- Ask the children to shut their eyes and smell different foods such as chocolate, orange, cheese and honey. Can they tell what it is just by the smell? Afterwards they can eat the food to check they got it right!

- Discuss what it would be like if you couldn't smell anything. Talk about how it would affect your enjoyment of food. When would it be dangerous? When would you miss smelling? What would you be glad not to smell?